SpaceShipOne: Making Dreams Come
True
Tom Sibila
AR B.L.: 3.3
Points: 0.5   MG

SpaceShipOne
Making Dreams Come True

by Tom Sibila

Reading Consultant:
Timothy Rasinski, Ph.D.
Professor of Reading Education
Kent State University

Content Consultant:
Kaye LeFebvre
Vice President/Corporate Secretary
Scaled Composites, LLC

Red Brick™ Learning

Published by Red Brick™ Learning
7825 Telegraph Road, Bloomington, Minnesota 55438
http://www.redbricklearning.com

Library of Congress Cataloging-in-Publication Data
Sibila, Tom.
   SpaceShipOne: making dreams come true / by Tom Sibila; reading
consultant, Timothy Rasinski.
      p. cm.—(High five reading)
Includes bibliographical references and index.
   ISBN 0-7368-5744-3 (soft cover)—ISBN 0-7368-5734-6 (hard cover)
   1. SpaceShipOne (Spacecraft)—Juvenile literature. 2. Aeronautics—United
States—Records—Juvenile literature. 3. Space flights—Juvenile
literature. 4. Rutan, Burt—Juvenile literature. I. Title. II. Series.

TL782.5.S53 2006
629.133'38—dc22
                              2005010095

Created by Kent Publishing Services, Inc.
Designed by Signature Design Group, Inc.
Edited by Jerry Ruff, Managing Editor, Red Brick™ Learning
Red Brick™ Learning Editorial Director: Mary Lindeen

Photo Credits:
Cover, pages 6, 8/9, 16, 17, 24/25, 27, 30, 36, Scaled Composites; page 4,
Hector Mata, Agence France Presse; page 10, Toronto Star Archive, Zarchive,
ZTSTAR; page 12, Robyn Beck, Agence France Presse; page 14, Lesley Ann
Miller, Zuma Press; pages 22, 32, Robert Galbraith, EPA Photos; page 28,
Associated Press, A/P; pages 38, 41, PA Photos; pages 42/43, Larry W. Smith,
EPA Photos

Printed in the United States of America.

1 2 3 4 5 6 11 10 09 08 07 06 05

Table of Contents

Chapter 1: Dream Vacation 5

Chapter 2: The Ansari X Prize 11

Chapter 3: June 21, 2004 23

Chapter 4: Going for the X Prize . . . 33

Chapter 5: Space Tourism 39

Epilogue 42

Glossary 44

Bibliography 46

Useful Addresses 47

Internet Sites 47

Index 48

A new day begins in the Mojave Desert.

Dream Vacation

This is your dream. Only a lucky few have done it. You wonder, "What will it feel like? Will I make it back alive? Is it worth the risk?"

Training

It is 6:00 a.m. You can't sleep. You look out the window. The **resort** is quiet. The sun rises in the desert sky. You rub your eyes. This does not feel like a vacation.

You check your watch. Training starts in two hours. First, doctors will check your health. Then, they will strap you into a machine. This machine will spin you so fast your cheeks will press back.

"Am I nuts?" you ask yourself.

---

resort (ri-ZORT): a place people go on vacation

You are strapped in a spaceship—waiting. In seconds, you will be pushed back into your seat. Your craft will climb higher and higher. What does your stomach feel like?

Five Days Later

Okay, now your fear is real. The straps are tight against your chest. Your ship is 45,000 feet (72,419 kilometers) in the air. You hear the countdown.

"5, 4, 3, 2, 1, release!"

Whoa! You feel a sudden drop. A rocket roars. The force slams you against your seat. Your cheeks press back again. You climb faster than a bullet.

You look out the window. The sky is blue. Then, it turns **indigo**. Eighty seconds later, it turns black. The rocket shuts down. There is no sound.

Your dream just came true. You are in outer space.

---

indigo (IN-di-goh): a dark, violet-blue color

What a View!

Your ship rolls to the left. Out your window, Earth comes into view. You can see 1,000 miles (1,609 kilometers) any way you want to look. Earth looks beautiful against the black sky.

Suddenly, it hits you. You are weightless. You take a lucky medal out of your pocket. You let the medal go. It floats!

Touchdown

A few minutes later, your craft heads down. Slowly, you glide back to Earth. Your ship touches down at the space resort. But your vacation is not over yet. Tonight, you will go to a party. There, you will be given your astronaut wings.

Could this happen to you? The answer might surprise you.

This is your view from space as you look out beyond the southern California coast.

Charles Lindbergh set a record when he flew this plane without stopping from New York to Paris.

Chapter 2

The Ansari X Prize

*In the early 1900s, most people never dreamed about flying. Only the rich or **reckless** might try. But one man dreamed that all people could fly.*

A Record Flight

In 1919, Raymond Orteig (or-TEEGH) offered a $25,000 prize. To win, a person had to fly a plane nonstop from New York to Paris. Many people tried. All failed.

Finally, in 1927, Charles Lindbergh went for the prize. Flying *The Spirit of Saint Louis*, Lindbergh made it! He won the $25,000. His flight made others believe that they could fly, too.

---

reckless (REK-liss): not careful; willing to take chances

Anousheh and Amir Ansari gave a large sum of money to help pay for the X Prize. The name of the prize was changed to the Ansari X Prize.

Another Big Dream

Today, planes full of people fly everywhere. Now, we have a new **frontier**—space travel. Could space travel be open to everyone?

Some people believe it can. In 1996, a group offered a $10 million prize to give **public** space travel a boost. To win the prize, a **private** group had to fly a **manned** craft into space and return safely. The prize was called the X Prize.

The X Prize had other rules, too. The winning craft had to make the flight twice in two weeks. Also, the craft had to carry the weight of at least three people.

Burt Rutan took up the challenge.

---

frontier (fruhn-TIHR): something that people are beginning to understand
public (PUHB-lik): open to everyone
private (PRYE-vit): not run by the government
manned (MAND): with people onboard

Burt Rutan believed his company, Scaled Composites, could build and fly a spaceship to win the X Prize.

Ticket to Ride

At the time, the U.S. government also was working on public space travel. The government office **NASA** said it would take at least 30 years. Rutan was 60 years old. He didn't want to wait that long.

Rutan said, "The first choice was to give up. Admit I would never go into space. [I would] never see that black sky. The other choice was to do something about it."

Rutan had a small company. He believed his company could build and fly a craft into space. He dreamed of space travel for all people. He decided to try to make his dream come true.

NASA: short for *National Aeronautics and Space Administration*

White Knight

First, Rutan designed a special jet plane. He built it to carry a small spacecraft on its belly. The jet could fly high into the air. From there it would drop the spacecraft.

Rutan named his jet *White Knight*. Its wings were 93 feet (28 meters) long. This would let the plane fly very high. The jet **cockpit** could hold three people.

White Knight

---

cockpit (KOK-pit): the area where the pilot sits

SpaceShipOne

Next, Rutan worked on the spacecraft.
He shaped the spacecraft cockpit like a bullet.
This allowed the wings to safely fold back.
It would make the craft safer coming down.
Rutan gave the craft a rocket engine.
He named his craft *SpaceShipOne*.

SpaceShipOne

The Funny Part

For fuel, Rutan wanted something that did not cost much and was safe. He chose **liquid** rubber and **nitrous oxide**. Nitrous oxide is also known as "laughing gas." It makes you feel silly if you breathe it. The nitrous oxide would **ignite** the rubber and make it burn. This would power the rocket.

---

liquid (LIK-wid): a wet substance that you can pour
nitrous oxide (NYE-tris AHK-side): a colorless gas
ignite (ig-NITE): to set fire to something

SpaceShipOne

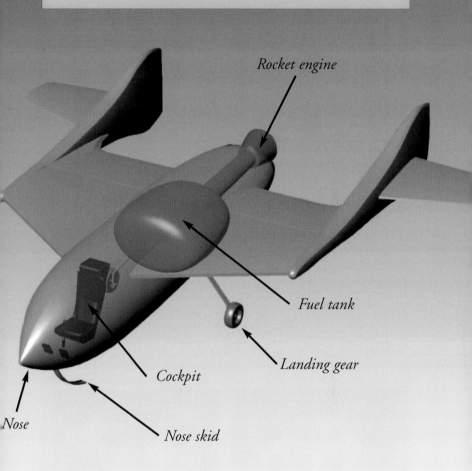

Rocket engine

Fuel tank

Landing gear

Cockpit

Nose

Nose skid

Coming Down

To come down, the pilot would move the wings to an angle. This would make the ship drop out of space. Pilots might feel 5 **G's** of force during this drop. Most roller coasters have G forces of 3.5 or less.

Next, the pilot would straighten the wings. The craft would begin to **glide**. It would circle down to Earth. Then the pilot would turn the craft to face the runway. It could then glide to a safe landing. Rutan's plan sounded great. But would it work?

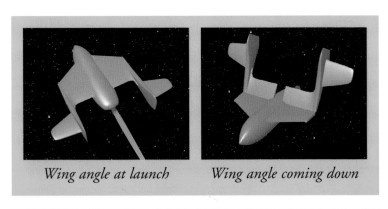

Wing angle at launch   *Wing angle coming down*

G (JEE): as something goes faster, it creates force; we can measure that force in G's.
glide (GLIDE): to fly without the power of an engine

Burt Rutan's Planned Flight Path of *SpaceShipOne*

3. *At 62.14 miles (100 kilometers), SpaceShipOne is in outer space.*

2. SpaceShipOne's rocket fires to send the craft up.

1. White Knight *drops* SpaceShipOne *at 50,000 feet (15,240 meters).*

4. *The pilot folds SpaceShipOne's wings to start down.*

5. SpaceShipOne drops toward Earth.

6. *At 80,000 feet (24,384 meters), the pilot levels SpaceShipOne's wings. The craft begins to glide.*

7. SpaceShipOne circles in for a landing.

Mike Melvill boards SpaceShipOne.

Chapter 3

June 21, 2004

Mike Melvill holds his lucky horseshoe. He gave it to his girlfriend when she was 16. One year later, they married. That was 43 years ago. Today, Melvill hopes it will give him luck. He also hopes to make history.

Runway 30

It is early morning at the Mojave Airport. *White Knight* slowly moves to runway 30. *SpaceShipOne* hangs under the plane. Melvill looks out the spacecraft's window. People are cheering for him. He opens a small window and waves.

Pilot Brian Binnie turns *White Knight* onto the runway. The jet picks up speed. At 6:47 a.m., *White Knight* lifts off.

Waiting

White Knight slowly climbs for one hour. Melvill sits in *SpaceShipOne*. He has little to do. He thinks about the flight he will soon take. "It's a pretty lonely time," he later says.

White Knight *carries* SpaceShipOne *high enough for launch.*

Finally, Binnie calls out a **checklist**. Melvill gets busy. He does each step on the list. A short countdown begins. Then Binnie lets *SpaceShipOne* go. It drops from the plane. About one second passes. Melvill hits the fire switch. The rocket ignites.

checklist (CHEK-list): a list of actions to be done

Climbing, Then a Problem

Three G's slam Melvill against his seat. "We're really hauling the mail," he says later. "You get the feeling that if you do anything wrong there, you might really hurt yourself."

Then something does go wrong. The craft rolls to the left. Melvill stomps on the **rudder** pedal. Now the craft rolls too far right. Melvill fights to straighten it. He reaches for a switch. One pull on this switch will shut the rocket off. Luckily, *SpaceShipOne* straightens out. Melvill doesn't have to pull the shut-off switch.

---

rudder (RUH-dur): a flap at the end of an aircraft used for steering

Can the Craft Make It?

The craft flies smoothly now. But the rolls created another problem. *SpaceShipOne* isn't flying straight up. This means it will take longer to reach outer space. Is there enough fuel to get there?

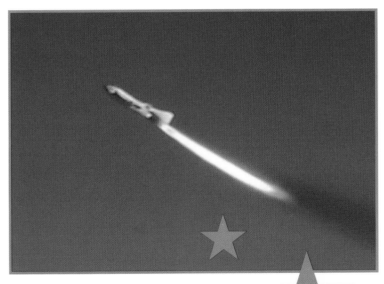

SpaceShipOne *rockets up toward space.*

Into Outer Space

The rocket burns for 75 seconds. Then it shuts down. Melvill is just over 62 miles (100 kilometers) above Earth. He has made it to outer space. He also has made history. At age 63, he is the first private astronaut.

Having Some Fun

Melvill is now weightless. He takes some M&M's® from his flight suit pocket. He opens his hand. The candy floats around the cockpit. "They just spun around like little sparkling things. And I was so blown away. I couldn't even fly the airplane," Melvill said later.

Mike Melvill in the cockpit of SpaceShipOne

Where Does Space Begin?

Most people agree that space begins where Earth's **atmosphere** ends. But the atmosphere thins out over hundreds of miles. So when are you really in space?

- The U.S. Department of Defense says space begins 50 miles (80.5 kilometers) above Earth.

- At 62 miles (100 kilometers), the air is so thin the sky looks black. Some say space begins here. The X Prize Foundation used this point, too.

- **Gravity** still pulls **satellites** from orbit at 110 miles (177 kilometers) above Earth. Are satellites really in space?

atmosphere (AT-muhss-fihr): the gasses around a planet
gravity (GRAV-uh-tee): the force that pulls things down toward Earth
satellite (SAT-uh-lite): a spacecraft sent into orbit around Earth, another planet, or some object in space

The Return

Melvill gets ready to return. He moves the wings. The craft begins to drop back into Earth's atmosphere. Next, he straightens the wings. Slowly, the craft glides down. At 9:14 a.m, he lands.

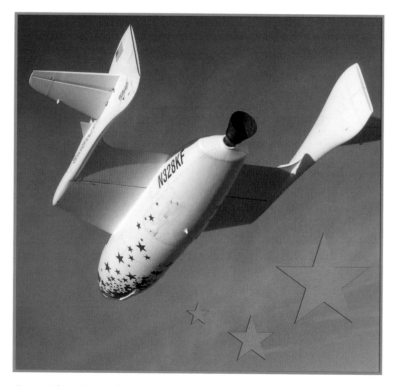

SpaceShipOne *glides in for a landing. The craft had just reached space for the first time.*

"Wow!"

Melvill steps out of *SpaceShipOne*. He hugs his wife. Astronaut Buzz Aldrin steps up to shake Melvill's hand. Aldrin was the second man to walk on the moon!

Later Melvill says, "It was very exciting. I must say I wasn't scared...all the way up. But I was a little afraid on the way down.... You know, you begin to believe, wow, should I really be doing this?"

Going for the Prize

Rutan had proved that a small company could send a person into space. Now, could he do it twice within two weeks? Only then could he claim the X Prize.

*Mike Melvill, Burt Rutan, and Brian Binnie
plan for the next flight.*

CHAPTER 4

Going for
the X Prize

SpaceShipOne *had made its first flight into space.*
Burt Rutan's team learned a lot from that flight.
They fixed the problems the flight had. Three months
later, they were ready. They would go for the X Prize.

September 29, 2004

Mike Melvill again sits in the cockpit of
SpaceShipOne. He thinks about his last
flight to space. *White Knight* climbs higher
and higher. Then Melvill hears the checklist.
The ship drops. The engine roars. He blasts
straight up.

More Problems

Melvill later talked about that launch.
"(I) started pulling back on the stick...
and [*SpaceShipOne*] just went straight up.
I couldn't believe how straight it was.
Last time, I was all over the sky."

People on the ground are yelling, "Go!
Go! Go!" The rocket is supposed to burn
for 88 seconds. Melvill hopes to reach 64.5
miles (103.8 kilometers) above Earth.

But the flight doesn't stay perfect for long.
After only 50 seconds, *SpaceShipOne* begins
to roll. Rutan says, "This was not planned
for." For about 60 seconds, the craft rolls.
It rolls five, 10, 15, 20 times. Melvill is
in trouble. "Come on, Mike!" someone on
the ground **pleads**.

---

plead (PLEED): to beg; to ask in a serious way

Shut Down

Doug Shane, the **flight director**, tells Melvill to shut down the engine. The rocket only burned for 76 seconds. Will that get Melvill into space?

SpaceShipOne keeps climbing. Melvill uses the rudders to straighten the craft. He starts to feel weightless. Now he uses the **thrusters** to stop the roll. The roll slowly stops. He reaches 63.9 miles (102.8 kilometers) above Earth. He is in space!

Melvill lands *SpaceShipOne* 23 minutes later. *SpaceShipOne* has not won the X Prize yet, though. It must make two flights in two weeks to win.

---

flight director (FLITE duh-REK-tur): the person on the ground in charge of a flight
thruster (THRUHST-ur): a small rocket that shoots gas; it is used to move a ship in space

October 4, 2004

Five days later, Rutan is ready to launch again. This time, Melvill calls out the checklist. He is the pilot for *White Knight*. Brian Binnie sits alone in *SpaceShipOne*.

"5, 4, 3, 2, 1, release." Binnie hits the switch. The rocket roars. For 84 seconds, the rocket burns. Then its fuel is gone. *SpaceShipOne* still climbs for almost a minute. Then it **levels off**.

Brian Binnie gets ready to fly SpaceShipOne.

---

level off (LEV-uhl AWF): to stop rising or falling and stay the same

"A Fantastic Feeling!"

Binnie flies *SpaceShipOne* to 69.6 miles
(112 kilometers) above Earth. He spends
about four minutes in space.

Then it is time to return. Binnie angles
the wings. The craft drops back toward
Earth. At 9:15 a.m., he lands.

Rutan's team has won the X Prize! Melvill
does a **flyby** in *White Knight.* The crowd
cheers. Later, Binnie talks about the flight.
"It's a fantastic view. It's a fantastic feeling.
There is a freedom there and a sense of
wonder that—I tell you what—you all
need to experience."

So, are you ready to travel to outer
space? Your chance may come sooner
than you think.

---

flyby (FLYE-bye): when a plane flies close to the ground so
people on the ground can see it better

Sir Richard Branson shares the news that his company plans to develop the world's first spaceliners.

— Chapter 5 —

Space Tourism

Your trip is over. You are flying back home. You look out the window of the jet. Somehow, Earth does not look the same. Reaching in your pocket, you pull out your wings. You think, "I really am an astronaut."

The Magic of Space

Since 1961, there have been about four manned space flights per year. The U.S. and Russian governments made most of those flights. However, in 2004, Burt Rutan's team made three flights.

Rutan wants space travel to be open to everyone. "I want…my kids and hundreds of thousands of people [to] experience the magic of space," he says.

All Aboard!

Rutan's dream may come true. Sir Richard Branson owns an airline in England. Sir Richard hired Rutan's company to build "spaceliners" like *SpaceShipOne*. Sir Richard hopes 3,000 people will become astronauts in five years. Within 15 years, he hopes 50,000 people will travel to outer space.

Are you ready to go? The price will be high at first—about $200,000. So far, more than 11,000 people have signed up. Maybe it is best to wait a few years. Rutan hopes that one day a ride into space will be as low as $5,000.

Fasten your seat belt.

"5, 4, 3, 2, 1, release!"

Sir Richard Branson and Burt Rutan hope to fly passengers into space by 2007.

Epilogue

Record Set

Some people call Burt Rutan "the world's greatest airplane designer." *SpaceShipOne* was not the first aircraft he built. Rutan also built *Voyager*. In December 1986, this plane flew nonstop around the world without **refueling**. No plane had ever done that before. The flight lasted a little over nine days. Rutan's brother Dick and Jeana Yeager flew *Voyager*. The record lasted for 19 years.

---

refueling (ree-FYOO-uhl-ing): filling with fuel again

Record Broken

Voyager's record was broken on March 3, 2005, by *GlobalFlyer*. This plane was flown by only one pilot, Steve Fossett. It took Fossett just under three days to fly *GlobalFlyer* nonstop around the world without refueling.

Can you guess who helped Fossett break the record? Burt Rutan designed *GlobalFlyer*. Sir Richard Branson helped pay for it!

GlobalFlyer *comes in to land. The plane had just made the first solo, nonstop flight around the world.*

Glossary

atmosphere (AT-muhss-fihr): the gasses around a planet

checklist (CHEK-list): a list of actions to be done

cockpit (KOK-pit): the area where the pilot sits

flight director (FLITE duh-REK-tur): the person on the ground in charge of a flight

flyby (FLYE-bye): when a plane flies close to the ground so people on the ground can see it better

frontier (fruhn-TIHR): something that people are beginning to understand

G (JEE): as something goes faster, it creates force; we can measure that force in G's.

glide (GLIDE): to fly without the power of an engine

gravity (GRAV-uh-tee): the force that pulls things down toward Earth

ignite (ig-NITE): to set fire to something

indigo (IN-di-goh): a dark, violet-blue color

level off (LEV-uhl AWF): to stop rising or falling and stay the same

liquid (LIK-wid): a wet substance that you can pour

manned (MAND): with people onboard

NASA: short for *National Aeronautics and Space Administration*

nitrous oxide (NYE-tris AHK-side): a colorless gas

plead (PLEED): to beg; to ask in a serious way

private (PRYE-vit): not run by the government

public (PUHB-lik): open to everyone

reckless (REK-liss): not careful; willing to take chances

refueling (ree-FYOO-uhl-ing): filling with fuel again

resort (ri-ZORT): a place people go on vacation

rudder (RUH-dur): a flap at the end of an aircraft used for steering

satellite (SAT-uh-lite): a spacecraft sent into orbit around Earth, another planet, or some object in space

thruster (THRUHST-ur): a small rocket that shoots gas; it is used to move a ship in space

Bibliography

Ackroyd, Peter. *Escape from Earth: Voyages Through Time*. New York: Dorling Kindersley, 2004.

Beyer, Mark. *Space Exploration*. High interest books: Life in the Future. New York: Children's Press, 2002.

Dyson, Marianne J. *Home on the Moon: Living on a Space Frontier*. Washington, D.C.: National Geographic, 2003.

Goldsmith, Mike. *Space Travel: Spinning Through Space*. Jordan Hill, Ill.: Raintree, 2001.

Useful Addresses

Scaled Composites
1624 Flight Line
Mojave, CA 93501

Smithsonian National Air and Space Museum
(On the National Mall)
6th and Independence Ave., SW
Washington, D.C. 20560

Smithsonian National Air and Space Museum
(Udvar-Hazy Center)
14390 Air and Space Museum Parkway
Chantilly, VA 20151

Internet Sites

National Aeronautics and Space Administration
http://www.nasa.gov

Scaled Composites
http://www.scaled.com/projects/tierone

Smithsonian National Air and Space Museum
http://www.nasm.si.edu

Virgin Galactic
http://www.virgingalactic.com

Index

Aldrin, Buzz, 31

Binnie, Brian, 23, 25, 36–37

Branson, Sir Richard, 40, 43

Fossett, Steve, 43

G force, 20

GlobalFlyer, 43

Lindbergh, Charles, 11

Melvill, Mike, 23–26, 28–31, 33–37

NASA, 15

nitrous oxide, 18

Orteig, Raymond, 11

Rutan, Burt, 13,15–18, 31, 33–34, 36–37, 39–40, 42–43

Rutan, Dick, 42

Shane, Doug, 35

SpaceShipOne, 17–21, 23–31, 33–37

Spirit of Saint Louis, The, 11

Voyager, 42

White Knight, 16, 23–24, 33, 36–37

X Prize, 13, 31, 33, 35, 37

Yeager, Jeana, 42